THE MEANING OF MY DREAM

UNLOCKING THE POWER OF DREAM INTERPRETATION

MIZ MZWAKHE TANCREDI

CONTENTS

ONE
THE PARALYSIS OF PROGRESS

"All human beings are also dream beings. Dreaming ties all mankind together."

– Jack Kerouac

Imagine a life where you could not tell what is real from what is not real, where you were unable to distinguish whether you were in a dream, or if what you were seeing was a waking reality. And the only way you could distinguish between a dream and reality was by the presence of a token that you must recognize both in the dream and when you are awake. Then, to add another layer of complexity, imagine that everything that happens in your life depends on recognizing or not recognizing the significance of the dream.

This is the concept behind the movie *Inception*, a mind-bending masterpiece about the multi-dimensional dream world and its effect on everything. Dom Cobb, the lead character, is a masterful thief who is skilled in the art of extraction. Cobb specializes in stealing valuable secrets from his victims when they are asleep and most vulnerable. But this is no ordinary kind of theft. He does not steal from their houses or safes. He steals from their minds.

Cobb is sought-out globally in his field, and an expert in his craft. The pivot of the movie happens when he is posed with the challenge of using his talent in the reverse direction. Instead of extracting a thought or idea from the mind, he is tasked with the seemingly impossible challenge of planting "a simple little idea that would change everything." The "back door" to gain access to the targeted person's vulnerable mind is to infiltrate their subconscious mind while they are in a sleep state.

Manipulating information using "back door" access is not as far-fetched as it sounds. In the world of information technology, this is done all the time. There is something called back-door programming. It is a way that the programmer can communicate with the operating system and execute instructions just in case he cannot gain access via the program's normal functioning. God, the Master Programmer, has also given Himself a back door entry point into your subconscious mind. In so doing, He can execute instructions that you are unable or unwilling to hear the way He originally intended. It is a special encrypted key, a token, as it were, that allows Him to communicate with you when preferred methods are not being utilized. We call this encrypted key a dream.

Dreams are a universal similarity. A universal similarity is something that is a shared common experience no matter who you are or where you come from. No matter where you are in the world, it is understood that we all have certain similar capabilities. For example, we laugh. We cry, even if only at certain times in our lives. These similarities are not specific to the physical realm only. There are also universal similarities that are spiritual. The word 'hallelujah,' for example, is a universal expression of praise. Though it may be spelt differently based on the location of the person using it, it is pronounced virtually the same way anywhere in the world. It is as though God has placed these special, shared experiences in our lives to validate our connectedness with Him and He with us. Universal similarities are designed to never be ignored.

There is another universal similarity that we will explore to an extent in this book. It is unique in that it is both physical and spiritual in nature. This universal similarity is that *everybody dreams*. The question is, *why?* Before we explore the answer to that question, and without getting into too many technicalities, we will examine a few simple facts about sleep and dreams.

People generally think of sleep as the part of their day where their activities end. They could never be further from the truth. Sleep is not the cessation of activity. It is, in fact, one of the most active times of your day, both physically and spiritually. First, we will deal with the natural, then the spiritual. Your brain is very active while you are asleep – it is not just resting. And if you do not get sleep, you do not function on a number of levels the way you should.

Physiologically, sleep is the state your body enters into during which brain-wave activity changes and your nervous system is less reactive to external stimuli. In other words, while you are asleep, you temporarily lose physical consciousness. God created you to have dominion, not only when you are awake, but also while you are sleeping. Suppose you do not understand how to take control of your sleeping and dreaming while you are not physically conscious. In that case, you will find yourself in one of the most vulnerable states you can be in both while you are asleep, and then after you wake up.

Your sleep is not constant throughout the night. You actually cycle through four distinct sleep phases multiple times. There are two stages of light sleep, then there is deep sleep. Lastly, there is rapid eye movement or REM sleep, which is when you dream. In the stages of light sleep, you can be awakened easily. Your consciousness is decreased, but your brain is still processing some information around you. It is in the initial light stage of sleep that someone can call your name without shouting, and you will immediately wake up. In the secondary or intermediate stage of light sleep, it is a little harder to wake you.

The deep sleep stage is the deepest, most restful, and most restorative stage of sleep. It is also the hardest stage from which to awaken. The brain is most active during this stage of sleep. It rewires itself and maps trillions of brain cells to new information you have learned. This is how you are able to process and retain new information you may have learned throughout the day. But this is only the start of the most significant activity that happens while you are asleep.

Dreams, the kind of dreams that we are discussing in this book, can happen at any time during sleep. But you have your most vivid dreams during the REM sleep stage. I alluded earlier to the fact that while you are asleep, you are in a very vulnerable state. That is because during REM, the brain is very active, and dreams are at their most intense. But during this most dream-filled phase of sleep, the voluntary muscles of your body — arms, legs, fingers, anything that is under conscious control — become paralyzed. This happens to prevent your body from acting out what is going on in the brain. You are the least physically conscious in this stage. However, this paralysis is intended for your progress. Because while your body and conscious mind are still, your spirit is in motion, actively participating in your dreams.

You may be one of the many people who believe that you do not dream when you sleep. It is not that you do not dream. You do dream, it's just that your message is being hijacked in the realms of the spirit. Everybody dreams every time they sleep. In fact, researchers have found that people usually have several dreams each night, each one typically lasting between five to twenty minutes. The problem is that most dreams are forgotten. As much as 95% of all dreams are quickly forgotten shortly after waking. There is a failure, a weakness in your spiritual circuitry, that does not allow you to recall the activity that took place in the dream. The dream realm is a spiritual realm in which your spirit is fully engaged. The strength of your spirit determines how much information your subconscious mind can hand over to your conscious mind after waking.

Another interesting fact which should never be ignored is that we spend roughly one-third of our lives sleeping. That means that by the time you reach the age of 60 years old, you would have spent twenty years in dreamland. Twenty years is nearly 240 months. That is equivalent to about 1,042 weeks, which is 7300 days or 10,512,000 minutes. If you are dreaming a third of your life away, you should have something to show for it. For that investment of time, you should understand how to get a profitable return from your dreams.

I do not want you to be an ignorant believer where the only thing you know is the door of your church and the colour of your Bible. You must reach a certain dimension where you understand the significance of your dreams - what they are, how they work, and how to use them to your advantage. Understanding dreams and being able to interpret what they mean brings spiritual growth. As a believer, somebody may come to you and say, I dreamt this or I dreamt that. They come to you believing that there is something you have that qualifies you to be able to tell them the meaning. But how can you tell them the meaning of their dream if you cannot even understand your own dreams?

Whether you realize it or not, you are living your dream life. You see, a dream is like a movie. God is involved in your dreams, but not the way you think. You are the director of your dreams, not God. It is you who chooses the cast and determines the role each character plays. You are manipulating your dreams. But if you do not understand the importance of your dreams and their purpose in your life, you will manipulate them in the wrong way. *Every dream is affecting your life, but you are not aware of it.* Therefore, you are not seeing and achieving what you desire.

There are those who do not have what you have, yet they are able to benefit from their dreams. Not only that, but you also are benefiting. Their dreams are controlling your life, and you were not even aware of it. In the next chapter, I will show you a few examples of this. I will begin to unravel the mystery of your dreams, and show you how to take your dream power back. Then you will go to sleep and dream and begin to accurately interpret the life you want and are supposed to have.

TWO
THE WISDOM OF DREAMS

"I dream of painting, and then I paint my dream."

– Vincent Van Gogh

The most human trait is to want to know why. That question motivates billions of people to seek answers to problems, dilemmas, questions, and other issues that make us wonder what is going on in the world. At the end of 2020, after analysing billions of search requests processed, it was discovered that "coronavirus" was the most searched word in the world. At the writing of this book, it still holds the #1 spot.

People want to understand "Why?" And the go-to source to find answers is the #1 search engine in the world, Google.

Google has become a household name. You would be hard-pressed to find any remotely Internet-savvy person who has not heard of or used the Google search engine. However, many people do not know how Google came into existence. Google was not the brainchild of a corporate board meeting, neither was it the result of years of research. The idea for Google was found in the middle of the night on the pillow of twenty-two-year-old Larry Page while he was fast asleep. The phenomenon we now know as Google was birthed out of a dream. What is even more interesting and of note is that his feelings of anxiety were the catalyst for this creative inspiration.

Page had an irrational fear that he would not be accepted to the college of his choice. In his own words, he describes what happened immediately after his vivid dream:

"When I suddenly woke up, I was thinking, *what if we could download the whole Web and just keep the links and ...?* I grabbed a pen and started writing."

Google was not the only creative, scientific, or inventive idea that came from an anxiety-induced dream.

Madam CJ Walker suffered a scalp infection that caused her to lose most of her hair. She went to sleep one night worried about her hair loss. In her dream, a man came to her and gave her the solution to her problem. This is her account of what happened.

"God answered my prayer, for one night I had a dream, and in that dream, a big Black man appeared to me and told me what to mix up for my hair. Some of the remedy was grown in Africa, but I sent for it, mixed it, put it on my scalp, and in a few weeks, my hair was coming in faster than it had ever fallen out. I tried it on my friends; it helped them. I made up my mind I would begin to sell it."

Madam CJ Walker's Wonderful Hair Grower made her the first Black American female to become a self-made millionaire.

I will share one more example to demonstrate the importance of dreams, understanding them, and acting upon them. If this next exemplary dreamer had failed to accurately interpret his dream, chances are you would not be sitting there in the clothes you are wearing right now.

Elias Howe, Jr. and his young family lived in poverty. His wife would mend other people's clothes, and he worked as an apprentice in a machine shop to try to earn enough money to make ends meet. He would sit and watch his wife sew for hours on end and wrestled for years to find a way to mechanise the movements of her hands as she sewed. Day and night, this problem troubled him until one night, he received the breakthrough he needed in a disturbing dream.

One night, after working fruitlessly on the problem, Howe fell into an exhausted sleep. He dreamed that he was building a sewing machine for a savage king in a far-off land. The king gave him twenty-four hours to complete the machine. But his dream mirrored his waking life, and he could not get it to work. The deadline passed, and the king's cannibal warriors came to execute him. If you don't know what cannibals are, those are people who don't see a person when they look at you. They see KFC or Nando's chicken. They are people eaters.

As the cannibals were preparing to cook him, they danced about waving their spears. He noticed that the spears had a hole at the end of the sharp tip. He immediately realised that was the solution for which he had been searching. Howe woke up with the idea to pass the thread through the point of the needle instead of at the end held by hand sewers. His was not the first sewing machine. It was, however, the first to come up with this innovative placement of the needle's eye. He was awarded the first American patent for a lockstitch sewing machine and eventually became a multi-millionaire.

Dreams are paramount. They have potentially life-changing natural and spiritual significance. And as we have seen in some of our examples, dreams are not only for believers. As long as you can sleep, you can dream. Dreams are for everyone, whether you are born again or not, whether you believe in God or not. The Bible attests to this fact.

In Genesis chapter 20, we have a fascinating account of how God used a dream to warn Abimelech, the king of Gerar. Abraham arrives in Gerar with his beautiful wife, Sarah, and tells King Abimelech that Sarah is his sister. The king takes one look at Sarah and says, *I've got to have this woman*! He wastes no time bringing Sarah to his royal court. But that night, God visits him in a dream and tells him, *if you don't give this woman back to her husband, you are a dead man.* Abimelech wakes up from the dream, loads up some gifts to give to Abraham, and sends Sarah packing!

Dreams can make you feel happy, sad, or as Abimelech found out, they can terrify you. And they may seem confusing or perfectly rational. Your emotions play a large part in the realm of dreams and their interpretation. Your dreams can be vivid, meaning you can experience a dream that is so real in the spiritual realm that it causes a manifestation in the physical realm. There is an interchange between what is happening in the natural and what is happening in the spiritual. I will give you a simple example to illustrate my point.

When I was growing up, there were times when I would dream that I was urinating. This was because, in the natural, I had a physical need to urinate. What was happening in the natural affected my dream. Then the dream caused a physical manifestation, and I would wake up in a wet bed. It was happening in the subconscious world. But at the same time, the conscious world was reacting to the subconscious world. That is the power of a dream.

Information about your physical, emotional, mental, and spiritual state is transmitted to your subconscious while you are asleep. But it takes command of the spiritual realm to pass the information you need from your subconscious to the physical realm after you wake up. In other words, you have to know what to do with your dream, how to interpret it after waking, and what next steps to take. Never take any dream lightly because dreams have meaning. Dreams are a way God uses to try to speak to us.

We are talking about dreams and their interpretation, but it is essential for you to understand that dreams are not God's ideal way of communicating with you. Sleep is generally relegated to a few hours at night. But God desires to communicate and fellowship with you in some form every minute of the day, not only when you are asleep. We are led by the Spirit, not by dreams. Why then do we concentrate on dreams? The answer is simple. God loves you, and He will use dreams as an avenue to communicate with you, sometimes as a last resort. God often uses dreams like a game of hide-and-seek. He wants to be found by you. He uses signs and symbols so that you are bound to seek Him to find the meaning of those dreams.

Not many people invest in their spiritual growth. Therefore, they are not at a level of maturity to catch what the Spirit of God is saying at any given time. You must be trained to know the Word of God more so that you do not rely solely on dreams. Dreams are the kindergarten of the spiritual realm. Still, there are fundamental principles that are vitally necessary that you can learn even at this basic level.

Most of the time, people dream and dream to the extent that they think their dreams are meaningless. Why does this happen? Because nothing that they see in a dream comes to pass. The enemy would like to convince you that a dream is just a dream and nothing more. Let me tell you something: there is no dream that is just a dream. Every dream has a meaning.

Sometimes God, through dreams, is trying to tell you what is happening around you. If things in your life do not seem to be working together for your good, it just may be that you are ignoring every sign God has given you in a dream. If you find that you have made some wrong choices or missteps, if you reflect, you may realise that there was a dream that God used to try to warn you before it happened. There are times in life where you get into so much trouble, and you do not know what to do. If you are not yet at a level where you can hear and understand His voice that is communicated through His Word and by His Spirit, God will always speak to you through dreams.

If you understood the importance of your dreams and how to interpret them, there would be fewer areas in your life in which you fall short. You would be able to recognise and avoid some of the things that you might do and later regret. It is evident that God speaks through dreams. But a dream is only as good as the level to which you can interpret it. You need to understand *why* you had the dream you had. There is a spiritual aspect to a dream and its interpretation. There is a skill aspect to it also. Where do you get this skill, and how does it work? Let's dig a little deeper into the dreamscape and find out.

THREE
DREAM KEYS

"The best way to make your dreams come true is to wake up."

– Paul Valery

The best time for a child to hear God is when he or she is not listening. I know you are wondering what I mean by that statement. I will explain. In the spiritual, just as in the natural, there are levels of growth and maturity. Spiritually, you can be a child (*nepios*) or a mature son of God (*teknon*). And your level of spiritual maturity affects how you see and perceive everything. This is what Apostle Paul means in the book of 1

Corinthians when he says, "When I was a child, I talked like a child; I thought or reasoned like a child; I *understood* like a child." But then he says, "When I became a mature man, I put away childish things." (1 Corinthians 13:11).

Your level of spiritual maturity also plays a vital role in your dreams: what you see and how you interpret what you see. Understand that God does not want you to be led by dreams. He wants you to be led by His Spirit. At the same time, He knows that His children are at varying levels of growth and maturity. Therefore, He has made it possible for any person to hear Him at any level of maturity using the vehicle of dreams. It is not His primary way of speaking to you, but it is a means of communicating with you, and one that should not be ignored. Therefore, it is paramount that you know how to interpret what you see in a dream.

When you are not spiritually immature, God has to wait until you are asleep to talk to you. There are Christians who have been born again for twenty years, but spiritually speaking, they are still in Pampers. It should not be that way. When you are first born again and a babe in Christ, it may start out like that. But as you mature in Christ – in the things of the Spirit and in the

Word of God – you grow from a baby (nepios) to a mature Christian (teknon).

When Samuel was a child growing up in the temple, He was unfamiliar with the voice of God. When God spoke to him, he could only interpret what he heard based on his limited knowledge and his surroundings. When Samuel heard the voice of God, he thought it was Eli the priest who was speaking to him. He had not yet reached a level of maturity that allowed him to discern and understand what God was saying, even when He spoke in a voice that was familiar. This happens many times in dreams. God will speak through what is familiar to you. But if you are a child spiritually, a *nepios*, you will interpret your dream based on your limited natural knowledge rather than your understanding of spiritual things.

Interpretation of dreams is not a gift. It is not something that you pray for, and the Holy Spirit comes and blows on you like a wind, and then you start interpreting dreams. It does not work quite like that. That does not mean that the Holy Spirit is not involved in the interpretation of dreams. He is very much involved. In fact, you cannot accurately interpret dreams that are inspired by God without the involvement of the Holy Spirit. Dream interpretation is by the Spirit of God *and* by skill. I want you to see how this worked in the life of Daniel.

In Daniel chapter 1, and verse 17, there is an interesting verse that will give you the first key to interpreting dreams. You cannot miss this. The Bible says:

As for these four children, God gave them knowledge and skill in all learning and wisdom: and Daniel had understanding in all visions and dreams. (Daniel 1:17)

There is so much in that verse. But let me pull out a few things from the text that you can put to work in the context of dream interpretation.

In this verse, the Bible is referring to Daniel and three other young men: Hananiah, Mishael, and Azariah. You may know them by their Babylonian slave names: Shadrach, Meshach, and Abednego. The text says that God gave them all knowledge and skill in all learning. They each had the ability to learn about any subject and gain mastery of it. The word "skill" there is the Hebrew word *sakal*. It means a special ability and intelligence to understand what other people do not understand. They were also given wisdom. It is not enough to know. You must also understand how to apply what you know. When you are given knowledge and understand it, then you are wise.

I want you to notice that there is a point of distinction between Daniel and the other young men. Though they were all endowed by the Spirit of God with the ability to learn and develop skill in any area, and with wisdom, Daniel took that ability a step further. He applied wisdom specifically to the area of dreams and visions and gained *understanding*. In other words, Daniel took what he had received from the Spirit of God and applied it to his understanding of dreams.

Interpretations belong to God. Your understanding of your dreams is based on one thing: what God says about the things you have dreamt. That is what differentiates your interpreting dreams from what psychics do. Your source is God. Never forget that. It is the Spirit of God who gives you the ability to understand what others cannot understand. Daniel became a master at interpreting all kinds of dreams. But notice it says Daniel "had" understanding, not he was "given" understanding. For you to interpret dreams accurately, you must do as Daniel did. Take what you receive from the Spirit of God through the Word of God. Then apply that knowledge to gain an understanding of your dreams.

You might be saying, "But I am not Daniel, and I was not given that skill. How can I interpret dreams?" Skill in all learning means dream interpretation can be taught. And if it can be taught, that means it can be learned. You have something superior to what Daniel had. You have the Holy Ghost inside you, the Master Teacher, the Spirit of Wisdom. And you have the Word of God. You also have the desire of God working in you to hear and understand Him, even if He is speaking to you in a dream. Let me remind you of what I said earlier. Dream interpretation is both by the Spirit of God and by *skill*.

Daniel had understanding in "all visions and dreams." That gives us another vital key to interpreting dreams. You must understand that there are different kinds of dreams and be skilled enough to recognize when a dream is coming from God and when it is not. All dreams are not created equal, and not every dream gives you a prophetic meaning. You can actually cause a dream through your own foolishness. I will show it to you in Jeremiah 29, verse 8:

For thus saith the Lord of hosts, the God of Israel; Let not your prophets and your diviners, that be in the midst of you, deceive you, neither hearken to your dreams which ye cause to be dreamed. (Jeremiah 29:8)

Let me repeat that last line in case you missed it. It says, "neither hearken to your dreams *which you cause to be dreamed.*" That is a powerful revelation! It is telling you two very crucial truths about dreams. First, dreams are caused by you. Remember, in the first chapter of this book, I told you that you are the director of your dreams, not God. You choose the cast and determine the role each character plays. You cause your own dreams by your environment, conversation, and spiritual input or lack thereof. What are you watching? What are you listening to? What do you indulge in? All these things create an environment that influences your dreams.

The other crucial point that Jeremiah 29, verse 8 reveals is that people around you can cause you to dream wrong dreams. In this verse, I want you to note that God is saying that people are encouraging the prophets to have the wrong dreams. If prophets who see what others cannot see and hear what others cannot hear can have their dreams influenced by other people, know that you are not exempt from this happening to you. Who are the people you talk to? Who do you surround yourself with? People around you can cause you to dream wrong dreams. And wrong dreams can never have right interpretations.

You can have an ordinary dream that is influenced by your environment. You know what I'm talking about. You remember that time when you stayed up late and watched that zombie movie, then you had a dream that zombies were chasing you around your room? Your dream was influenced by what you watched, your environment. An ordinary dream might be pointing to what is happening in your life and have nothing to do with your spiritual life. Or it may be a dream that warns you about something. God may be trying to show you people who are a bad influence in your life. When you take from the conscious world, good or bad, and bring it into the subconscious realm when you sleep, that is called an ordinary dream.

You can also have what is called an *ónar* dream, which is a prophetic dream. God has used dreams (ónars) to make important announcements in the Bible. For example, the Lord appeared to Joseph in an ónar. That dream announced the birth of Jesus, settling the confusion in his heart about taking Mary to be his wife (see Matthew 1:20). The instruction to preserve the life of Jesus as a young child was also given to Joseph in a dream (ónar). You will find that account in Matthew chapter 2, verse 13.

An ónar is directed to you. But it is important to note that an ónar can be influenced by a source that is not God. When it comes to the prophetic, it is not always the outcome that determines whether a prophecy is true or false. It is the source of the prophecy. You can have what appears to be a good dream, but it is coming from a bad devil.

For example, in Matthew 27, verse 19, Pilate's wife was troubled by a dream (ónar). That dream led her to try to convince her husband to let Jesus go so He would not be crucified. To the unskilled and non-Spirit led person, that might sound like a good dream. However, the dream was a direct attempt by the devil to keep Jesus from going to the cross, which directly opposed the will of God. That means you can have a dream that is prophetic, but it takes the Spirit of God and skilful use of the Word of God to determine if it is a prophetic dream that is coming from God.

The will of God is found in His Word. Apostle Paul says that babies—the spiritually immature—are unskilled in the Word of God. But the spiritually mature—those who are skilled in the Word—can discern both good *and* evil (Hebrews 5:13-14). You need to be able to discern both. The interpretation of a dream must be led by the Spirit of God *and skill*.

You can go to bed and dream that someone hands you the keys to a brand-new Lamborghini. But before the dream is over, you find yourself riding a donkey. Wake up from that dream and tell the devil, "You can keep your donkey. I will keep my Lambo!" Whenever you have a dream, always ask the Holy Spirit to help you to interpret the dream. He will ensure that the dream and your interpretation of it line up with the will of God and His purpose for your life. If it does not line up, rebuke it!

So, you can have an ordinary dream where you take what is in your environment and bring it into your subconscious world. Or you can have an ónar, which is a prophetic dream that is directed to you. But you need the Spirit of God and skill to determine its source. Then you can have an *enupnion*, which is a spiritual dream directed to people around you. We find mention of this in Acts chapter 2, verse 17:

And it shall come to pass in the last days, saith God, I will pour out of my Spirit upon all flesh: and your sons and your daughters shall prophesy, and your young men shall see visions, and your old men shall dream dreams

An enupnion is a spiritual suggestion. Watch what it says in Job chapter 33, and verses 14 to 15:

For God speaketh once, yea twice, yet man perceiveth it not. In a dream, in a vision of the night, when deep sleep falleth upon men, in slumberings upon the bed (Job 33:14-15)

Two things are mentioned here: a dream and a vision of the night. There is a big difference between a dream and a vision of the night. A vision tells you directly what it is. There is nothing to interpret or figure out. It is what it is. God's will is for you to have visions. We are not talking about visions. That is another book for another time. For now, it is enough to know that there is a difference between visions and dreams. Visions are plain, straightforward, and usually straight to the point. Dreams, on the other hand, are more symbolic. They are more cryptic than self-explanatory.

Job caught that revelation. He goes on to say that in dreams, God speaks once, yet you hear Him twice. How does God speak once, and you hear him twice? It is like an echo of His voice that, after speaking once, it reverberates from the spiritual to the natural realm. When you are in a deep sleep, you are no longer listening with your physical ears. The conscious mind and the physical body get quiet, and the subconscious spiritual realm becomes more active. Your subconscious mind is the ear of your spirit. It never stops listening.

So, God speaks once in a dream, while you are functioning in the subconscious realm. Then when you wake up and re-enter the conscious world, you are now thinking about what you saw in your dream and hearing His voice again. You heard Him twice, first in the subconscious, then in the conscious realm. The problem, Job points out, is when you do not perceive it. You must be able to interpret what God is saying to you in your dream.

Understand that there are about sixty-six methods of interpreting dreams. This book is not intended to be an exhaustive reference. But in the next chapter, I will show you certain dream themes that are very common across different cultures. Using some of these common dreams, you will have a starting point for understanding and interpreting your own dreams. I will make it as simple as possible.

FOUR

NUMBERS, COLOURS, ANIMALS AND THEIR MEANINGS

DEVELOPING YOUR DREAM INTERPRETATION SKILLS

"I dreamed I was a butterfly, flitting around in the sky; then I awoke. Now I wonder: Am I a man who dreamt of being a butterfly, or am I a butterfly dreaming that I am a man?"

— Zhuangzi

Your environment determines what you are going to dream. When we talk about an environment, we are not referring to your location only. We are talking about what surrounds you - the information, the people, the inspiration. Your environment is what makes you tick. Environment plays a crucial role because the things around you determine how you interpret the symbols in a dream.

Remember, dream symbols have two or more meanings to them. Do not ever forget that. With any dream interpretation, always start by asking the Holy Spirit to lead and help you. Secondly, use your skill, your knowledge of the Word of God and information you may already have about dream symbols. Do not rush to interpret things you do not understand. If a dream is too cryptic for you to interpret, it is best to leave it to those who are more skilled in interpretation.

Many people confuse the spiritual meaning of a dream symbol with its physical meaning. Context is everything. And dream interpretation is a skill that you need to keep practising. Use the following dream symbols and other widely accepted biblical symbols to help you as you begin to learn how to develop your dream interpretation skills.

Numbers

1: Symbolizes unity (see Philippians 2:2).

2: Symbolizes witness (see Matthew 18:20 and 2 Corinthians 13:1).

3: Symbolizes God as the triune God – Father, Son and Holy Spirit.

4: Symbolizes the Earth, e.g., 4 winds, 4 seasons, the 4 corners of the Earth (see Revelation 7:1).

5: Symbolizes God's enabling grace and power (see Leviticus 26:8).

6: Symbolizes the number of man (see Genesis 1:24, 31 and Revelation 13:18).

7: Symbolizes completeness or perfection (see Genesis 2:2). The number 7 is very prophetic.

8: Symbolizes new beginnings (see 1 Peter 3:20).

9: Symbolizes the Holy Spirit, e.g., the 9 fruit of the Spirit (see Galatians 5:22-23).

10: Symbolizes trial and testing (see Daniel 1:12-15).

Colours

Colours are very symbolic in dreams. These are base colours (also found in the colours of the rainbow). Always remember the context of the dream. Pay attention to what is happening in the dream and the details surrounding the symbolism you see.

Blue: Symbolizes revelation or authority from Heaven. It can also mean sadness (depending on the context and details of the dream).

Green: Symbolizes prosperity, life, or permission to move forward/the go-ahead (i.e., "I have the green light."

Orange: Symbolizes danger or warning.

Purple: Purple is the colour of royalty. It symbolizes Jesus as king and ruler.

Red: Symbolizes the Blood of Jesus, which translates to freedom and forgiveness. Red can also mean passion and anger.

Scarlet/Crimson: Symbolizes sin (see Isaiah 1:18).

White: Symbolizes purity (see Revelation 3:4).

Yellow: Symbolizes glory. It can also symbolize fear, or it can mean slow down or be cautious.

Remember, context is everything. If you do not examine the context of your dream, you can get the interpretation wrong altogether.

Modern-Day Transportation

Typically, though not all the time, modes of transportation represent churches or ministry.

Aeroplane: Symbolizes a church or ministry that moves in the Spirit. A large airliner usually symbolizes a large church. An aeroplane can also signify visions. It represents something that can travel far. It might mean that God is calling you into visions or that you need to pay attention to visions. It could symbolize open visions or closed visions. But in most cases, it means visions.

Battleship (anything related to war/military): Symbolizes spiritual warfare. Something is happening that is not right, and you are fighting.

Bicycle: Symbolizes too much effort when you should be allowing the Holy Spirit to work. A bicycle could also mean local evangelism.

Car: If you see yourself in a car or buying a car, it could mean individual (personal) or small ministry.

Driver looking in rearview: Symbolizes focusing

too much on the past.

Helicopter: Symbolizes dreams. You might not be paying attention to your dreams. Or you may need to pay closer attention to the dreams that you are currently having or the dreams you're going to have. It all depends on the context of the dream.

Moving truck: Symbolizes change or relocation. The one driving is usually the one in authority or in control.

Rowboat: Symbolizes ministry that relies on human effort for its success. It is important for you to make an effort, but the Holy Spirit must be your driving force.

School Bus: Symbolizes a childrens or teaching ministry.

Ship: Symbolizes church or ministry. If the ship is on the ocean, it could mean ministry to nations.

Tractor/Trailer/Truck: Symbolizes ministry that is bringing provision. A truck might also mean social development. God might be calling you to focus on community work either by doing charity work or anything that has to do with community development.

Train Station/Bus Depot/Docks/Airport/Parking Lot: Symbolizes a time of waiting or impending transition or moving in a different direction.

Vehicle stopping for fuel: Symbolizes the need to stop and refuel on the Word of God and prayer. It means you need to recalibrate spiritually.

Walking: Symbolizes soul-winning, especially when a person is walking fast.

Animals

Ants: Symbolize new opportunities. Ants in your dream might also mean a new job. Or it could represent too much work ahead.

Bees: Symbolizes good news. It's different if you see bees stinging you in the dream. If you see yourself being stung by bees, it might mean that you are being overwhelmed.

Deer: Symbolizes being under attack.

Donkey: Symbolizes hard work. It also represents a

lack of progress, or it could mean rejection.

Dragon: Symbolizes hope. It can also mean anger or frustration.

Eagle: Symbolizes a prophet or a prophetic office. Contrary to what many people believe, an eagle does not symbolize the prophetic. Every Christian can be prophetic, but that does not mean every Christian is a prophet. Similarly, every prophet is an intercessor, but not every intercessor is a prophet. Just because one is prophetic, it does not make them a prophet. But if you constantly see eagles in your dreams, it might be a sign that God is calling you into a prophetic office.

Elephant: Symbolizes loneliness. It could also mean political influence or authority.

Goat: Symbolizes a lack of direction.

Horse: Symbolizes prophetic speed. It could also mean spiritual warfare or an angelic encounter.

Lion: Symbolizes courage. Sometimes, depending on the context of the dream, it could mean that God is trying to show you that you need to work on your attitude. It also has to do with self-esteem. You might have high self-esteem, which can be good.

Monkey: Symbolizes betrayal. And it can also mean that you are concerned about the past, or that the past is coming to haunt you. It depends on what is happening in the dream.

General Symbols

Darkness: Symbolizes lack of spiritual light or vision.

Death of a person: This is not typically a bad thing. It could symbolize the death of the sinful pleasures of the flesh.

Door: Symbolizes opportunity.

Earthquake: Symbolizes God's power.

Electricity: Symbolizes the power of God.

Flower: Symbolizes natural beauty.

Map: Symbolizes God's direction.

Microwave: Symbolizes things happening quickly.

Moon: Symbolizes people of God. Christians do not have any light of their own. They are reflecting the glory of the Lord.

Photograph: Symbolizes a memory of the past.

Stains or dirt on your clothes: Symbolizes sin.

Sun: Symbolizes glory and the light of God.

Teeth: Symbolizes the ability to comprehend the Word of God.

————

All dreams are not created equal, and all dream symbols do not carry the same weight. Some dreams are more significant than others. Understanding that can make the difference between hearing God or ignoring Him altogether. In the next chapter, I will show you the only kind of dream where God speaks directly to you. If you miss this, you will miss everything.

FIVE

PROPHETIC DREAMS AND THEIR MEANINGS

"Every night is about a dream of purpose."

— Uebert Angel

In an earlier chapter, I mentioned three different kinds of dreams. You can have what is called an ordinary dream. An ordinary dream has no spiritual significance. We also have spiritual dreams and prophetic dreams, and there is a difference between the two. A spiritual dream is directed to people around you. It may be about your surroundings or other people around you – your family, siblings, etc. A spiritual dream could even be about a nation or a province. A spiritual dream is where God is talking about you or anything that concerns or surrounds you. A prophetic dream, on the other hand, is directed to you.

Accident: A car is symbolic of what moves you from one place to another. If you dream that you are involved in an accident, it does not necessarily mean you will wake up and have an accident. It also depends on who is driving the car in the dream. You can drive safely, but it does not mean that somebody cannot come and hit you. An accident may be symbolic of the outcome of a business, ministry, or relationship. It might also represent decisions that you're about to make. God may be warning you and directing you not to make that move or investment, or whatever the case may be.

Belt: Symbolizes confidence. A belt is also symbolic of a covenant or agreement. It also represents unity.

Cabbage: If you see cabbage in a dream, whether you are cooking it or harvesting it, cabbage is symbolic of increase in your life. Cabbage can also mean that too many people depend on you, or you are more focused on helping others rather than yourself. Many people who dream about cabbage will realize that their lives are being spent helping others, but nobody helps them in return. They are being strained, drained, or used by people who depend on them.

Castle: A castle symbolizes responsibility. If you see a castle in your dream, it could mean there is a greater work ahead of you. Something big is coming your way, and you need to prepare yourself.

Coffin (Seeing a Coffin): A coffin (i.e., seeing a coffin) symbolizes a new season or new people in your life. It is also symbolic of marriage. If you see a coffin falling, it could mean your marriage or a relationship might be falling. A coffin could also mean somebody is about to propose. Most people confuse the physical meaning of a thing and the spiritual meaning of a thing. This is a dream symbol whose interpretation won't make sense if you only consider the physical meaning of the symbol. We are talking about a prophetic dream. Therefore, you must consider the spiritual meaning of the symbol and what God is saying to you directly.

Cow: Cows symbolize different things depending on how the dream starts and ends. Cows can represent tribal spirits following you, such as spirits from your father's house. If you see cows chasing or harassing you, it means generational issues. If you see yourself taking care of cows, it could symbolize wealth. A cow also represents evangelism in the Spirit. It symbolizes harvest because cows are used to plough at harvest time. You might have entered a season of harvest, or God may be directing you to soul winning.

Death of a Person: Seeing the death of a person in a dream is different from seeing a dead person. In most cases, when you dream about the death of a person, it is someone that you know. You attend the funeral of somebody that you know. So, dreaming the death of a person symbolizes separation, something coming between you and someone you know. The thing that causes the separation could be a rumour or gossip. The main point is that the death of a person represents something that will cause separation.

Dogs: Symbolize people who are close to you. Dogs are symbolic of people, your surroundings, friends or family members. A dog is known to be man's best friend. So dogs in a dream represent people who are close to you. Again, it also depends on what is happening in the dream and what the dogs are doing. We will discuss the symbolism of dogs more in-depth in the next chapter.

Dove: A dove is a biblical symbol representing the Holy Spirit. A dove has two wings, and each wing has nine main feathers. The left wing represents the nine gifts of the Holy Spirit, and the right wing represents the nine fruit of the Spirit. A dove's tail has five feathers. The tail steers, provides lift, support, and balance. It also helps the dove to land. So, the tail of five feathers represents the five-fold ministry.

The five-fold ministry consists of apostles, prophets, evangelists, pastors, and teachers. One cannot function fully in the gifts of the Spirit and the fruit of the Spirit without following the five-fold ministries. Apostles, prophets, evangelists, pastors and teachers are there for the equipping of the saints. So, when you see a dove in your dream, it symbolizes spiritual growth or a relationship with the Holy Spirit. It may be God directing you to pursue walking in the fruit of the Spirit. You would also need to pay attention to what the dove is doing in the dream.

Faeces: Faeces could indicate that you are troubled or bothered. It could also mean the death of something valuable (e.g., a relationship, a job or work). Faeces could also symbolize people who are draining you that you need to eliminate from your life. It makes a difference if you only see faeces, or you are the one releasing them. If you are releasing yourself, it means you need to get rid of negativity in your life. That negativity might be your own mindset, words, or it could be negative people around you.

Fire: Fire could symbolize an argument or misunderstanding. If you see fire in your dream, you also need to note how the fire started. It might also represent confusion or a wrong turn. It could also indicate a warning. For example, you might have recently entered a new relationship. In that instance, seeing fire in a dream could mean God is warning you about that relationship.

Giving Birth: Symbolizes blessings. Giving birth is different from pregnancy (discussed below). Giving birth in a dream means you have just stepped into a season of joy. However, if you see yourself helping somebody give birth, God is saying that I want you to serve others in this season.

Hen: We spoke of cows which symbolize tribal spirits from your father's house. A hen represents tribal spirits following you from your mother's house. This indicates generational or bloodline curses. What conquered your mother is about to conquer you.

Mango: When you see yourself eating a mango, it usually symbolizes motion, movement, or making progress. The parts of the word provide a clue to its symbolic meaning: man go. When you see a green mango, it means you are about to start something (e.g., a business or a church), or you are entering into a new relationship. A green mango could also symbolize having the "green light" or the go-ahead to move forward in a decision or move that you are about to make. If you see a red mango, it means do not move forward, or it could mean be patient. If you see a yellow or orange mango, it symbolizes your need to prepare to move forward.

Mountain: A mountain symbolizes hindrances, challenges ahead that you need to prepare for, or obstacles you need to go around or over. A mountain could also represent a season of growth.

Nakedness: When you see yourself naked in a dream, it could symbolize shame, or it could represent freedom. When you are in your house on your own, you can dance naked or walk around naked. But if you realize that somebody has been watching, you might feel embarrassed or ashamed. So nakedness can symbolize secrets that you never wanted anybody to know about. It could mean those secrets are about to be exposed. Nakedness might also mean you have entered a season of freedom or rest.

Owl: An owl is a rare bird and a bird of the night. So, an owl could symbolize God's desire for you to rest. When one sees an owl in a dream, it might also mean God wants you to rest. Maybe you are working too hard, or you are not getting enough rest for whatever reason.

Some species of owls have two dark spots on the back of their head or neck that resemble eyes. Many owl species can turn their heads 270 degrees in either direction. So, an owl might also represent being watched. I once had a dream where an owl was watching me. When I turned and went behind the owl, it had what looked like eyes at the back. When I woke up, the immediate interpretation I had was that there is an evil spirit monitoring me, so I rebuked that spirit.

An owl could also mean promotion. It could also represent death, especially when someone is sick at home or in the hospital. Depending on the context of the dream, God may be directing you to rebuke death.

Pregnancy: Symbolizes you are about to birth something. It could be a baby or something else that is new. For example, you might be starting a new job, business or ministry. Or maybe you are writing a book. Pregnancy also represents development. It could also indicate that you are making progress; you are growing, moving from one stage to another.

Snake: Snakes do not always represent evil. For example, when you dream of a snake and its eggs, it could symbolize wealth. If you have ever been to a high-end store that sells snake-skin shoes, they are always expensive. A snake can also represent healing, recovery, or restoring something to its original form.

When the children of Israel were bitten by serpents in the desert, Moses was instructed to raise a bronze serpent where they could see it. When those who were bitten raised their eyes and gazed upon the snake, they were healed (see Numbers 21:6-9). We will discuss the symbolism of snakes in more detail in the next chapter, which discusses dangerous dreams.

Train: A train symbolizes a church that is steeped in tradition (i.e., concentrating too much on the way you are used to doing something). Tradition is frozen success. A train always takes the same route. It is very rigid and inflexible, with no room for the Spirit to move. A dream with such symbolism may mean that you need to let go and embrace the way God is moving you by the Spirit. You might be sitting inside a train in the dream, or you may be the one driving the train. Check that you are not stuck in tradition. On the flip side, a train in your dream could mean your ministry is continuously on the move and on track. Always check the context. What were you doing on the train? What was the feeling?

Valley: If you dream that you are in a valley, it represents you looking down on yourself or low self-esteem. Pride is when you put yourself in a position that you are not. But when God lifts you up, He expects you to be up but with a humble heart. Looking down on yourself is not humility. It is hypocrisy.

Wheelchair: If you see yourself in a wheelchair, it could mean you depend on other people to support you or cheer you on. You might be stagnant in your life. God may be trying to tell you that you rely too much on people emotionally. It may mean you need to take a stand and begin to get things done. People are not obligated to support you, believe in you, or stand with you. You need to do that for yourself.

———

You can dismiss or reject what you see in a dream once you discern that the source of the dream is evil. You may also rebuke what you have seen in a dream when you know it does not line up with God's will or purpose for you. No dream, however, should be ignored. And when you see a dream repeatedly, that indicates your need to pay attention to something you are supposed to be doing. A repeated dream is just one example of a dream that demands your attention. In the next chapter, I will reveal some of the most dangerous dreams you should never ignore.

SIX

DREAMS TOO DANGEROUS TO IGNORE

AND DREAMS INDICATING WITCHCRAFT ACTIVITY

"The interpretation of dreams is a great art."

— Paracelsus

Every activity in your life either contributes to your dreams or is affected by your dreams. The significance of dreams should not be understated. Major events in the Bible took place in dreams. In Genesis chapter 15, Abraham, the Father of Faith, entered into a covenant with God in a dream. In 1 Kings chapter 3, Solomon became the wisest man through His encounter with God. It happened in a dream. God Himself, in His reprimand of Aaron and Miriam, announced that dreams are one of His chosen means of communication (see Numbers chapter 12, verse 6). God has used dreams to provide instruction, opportunity, warnings, guidance, and blessings. God unequivocally speaks through dreams. But that does not mean that God is speaking through every dream.

Understanding that God does not speak through every dream should let you know that not every dream should be listened to. However, every dream should be understood, and that understanding starts with knowledge. Without knowledge, your dream life could destroy you. Dreams are heavily influenced by your personal experiences. To complicate matters, dreams are symbolic, and symbols can have multiple meanings. Without knowledge, you will misinterpret what you are seeing. What I am about to share will give you insight into some of the more common dreams and dream symbols.

Being Shot in A Dream

There are other dreams that serve as signs of witchcraft activity. One is when you see yourself being shot in a dream. The symbolism of being shot in a dream does not mean what you might think. It does relate to violence, but not the physical kind. You could dream that you are shot by an arrow or a gun, but being shot typically symbolizes financial hindrance. It means there is a spirit working against your progress financially.

In the olden days, when a person was enslaved by an oppressor, there was little the enslaved person could do about it. The oppressors had weapons, eventually guns, that could kill the slave in a split second. Those weapons brought fear to the one who was enslaved. The Bible gives us the spiritual significance of such imagery. Proverbs chapter 22 and verse 7 tells us that the borrower is a slave to the lender. That speaks of financial bondage. In other words, debt causes you to be a slave. If you see yourself being shot in a dream, it symbolizes an attack on your finances.

Chased By Dogs

A lot of people dream that they are being chased by dogs. On the surface, if you do not understand dream interpretation, being chased by a dog would appear to be troubling symbolism. But, if you have the knowledge to look deeper, you would see something else. Dogs are not as bad as you think. Dogs are known as man's best friend. Dogs are the most loyal animals. Therefore, dogs in a dream could symbolize a friend or friendship. Or they could represent people who are close to you, people you believe to be loyal and trustworthy, or your inner circle.

The Bible also warns us to beware of dogs. These are people who appear to be close but are working dissension and strife from within the ranks. Dogs can symbolize the loyalty of someone close to you. But bear in mind that the Bible says the enemy transforms himself into an angel of the light (see 2 Corinthians chapter 11, verse 14). That means there could be people who appear to be trustworthy who are not. Such people could also be symbolized as dogs in your dreams. So, you must pay attention to the context when you dream about dogs or any dream symbol. What were the dogs doing in the dream? Were they barking? Were they biting you? Or were they protecting you? Those kinds of details will help you to understand and interpret what you saw.

Drowning

Any dream that depicts you being harmed is disturbing. But always remember that dreams are symbolic, which means the interpretation differs based on the symbolism and the context. For example, water can symbolize different things. In a good dream, water could symbolize the peace of God. Or it could represent the Holy Spirit. The context of the dream – what is happening in the dream as well as the details – affects the way you would interpret it. Also, and very importantly, you need to pay attention to the feeling you have when you wake up from the dream. That plays a large part in how the dream is to be interpreted.

If you have a bad dream that you are drowning, then water in that context takes on a different meaning. Up to 60% of the human adult body is water. The brain and heart are 73% water, and the lungs are about 83% water. The skin contains 64% water, muscles and kidneys are 79%, and even the bones are watery: 31%. Symbolically, water can represent inner emotions. With that in mind, dreaming that you are drowning could signify drowning emotionally. For example, you feel overwhelmed by worry or anxiety because of something at work, at home, or in a relationship. Or it may be in some other area in your life.

Losing Blood

There are some dreams that you know are bad based on the activity in the dream. For example, you may see yourself bleeding in a dream. How you came to be bleeding may or may not be revealed in the dream. The mere fact that you see yourself losing blood is a symbol that should get your attention.

The Bible tells us in the book of Leviticus that the life of each and every animal is in the blood. Applying that knowledge, if you see yourself bleeding, it means death. In most cases, it symbolizes an accident. It can also symbolize losing a job. In general, if you are bleeding in a dream, it means something is losing life. Something is vulnerable, dying, or ceasing to exist in your life or in your world. Wake up and pray.

Nightmares

Any bad dream can be alarming. But the dreams most people dread the most are nightmares. Nightmares and bad dreams are not the same things. Both are disturbing dreams, but according to those who study sleep behaviours, only a nightmare will cause you to wake from sleep. As with all dreams, there is a spiritual component that most medical doctors do not know anything about. It is the spiritual aspect of a nightmare that you need knowledge about.

We know what night is. But what does the word 'mare' mean? The word 'mare' comes from a word that means 'goblin,' which is an evil spirit or demon. When you say you had a nightmare, you are saying you had a visitation from an evil spirit at night. Secular physicians and specialists will say that is superstition. While your mind might be tempted to believe that, your spirit will testify to the reality of it because after every nightmare, you are surrounded by fear. The Bible says that God has not given you the spirit of fear (2 Timothy 1, verse 7). We know that whenever or wherever fear dominates, God is not part of it. A nightmare is a dream that indicates witchcraft activity is happening in your life or in your family. That is not a dream to be ignored.

Snakes

Snakes in a dream are troubling symbolism for many people. And in certain instances, it should be. Snakes can symbolize deception. Remember what happened in Genesis chapter 3 when Eve was deceived by the snake. Three of the most notable characteristics of a snake is the movement of its tongue, the hissing sound the tongue makes, and, depending on the kind of snake, its venomous bite. All three are connected to the mouth.

The enemy moves in deception, and that deception is communicated in words. We see that even in the time of Jesus after He was baptized and led into the wilderness. The devil came to try to deceive Jesus and lead Him away from His purpose. That was the same thing he (using the serpent) did to Adam and Eve in the Garden of Eden. When you see snakes in your dreams, depending on the feeling and context of the dream, it could mean that someone is trying to hijack your destiny.

Bear in mind, your fears in the natural can cause you to describe what was a symbol of joy in the night. For example, you could dream of a snake and interpret it as deception, or a witch or witchcraft. But the reality is, God created the snake. He did not create a witch, and He has nothing to do with deception.

In Numbers 21, verse 9, the Bible says Moses lifted up the serpent in the wilderness. Later, in John chapter 3, verse 14, Jesus identifies Himself as the serpent that was lifted up. That means, in that context, the serpent symbolized Christ. Not only that, but the Bible also says we should be as wise as serpents (see Matthew 10:16). That means a serpent can symbolize wisdom. The mind that is renewed by the Word of God will interpret symbols differently. Here is another example of that.

Trapped

Any dream in which some form of control is used against you, whether directly or indirectly, is a dangerous dream. For example, if you dream that you are trapped, you should never ignore such a dream. In the dream, you could be trapped in a house, a school, a car, or wherever it may be. The bottom line is, you cannot get out. You try your best to move, but you cannot. You feel trapped. What does that dream mean? It means that somebody is attacking you. And this is no simple attack. This is an attack of words. Somebody is speaking ill or evil against you.

That is not a dream you can wake up and be passive about. That is a dream you must wake up and do something about. In Isaiah chapter 54, verse 17, the Bible says, "no weapon formed against you shall prosper." But it does not end there. It goes on to say, "every tongue that shall rise against you shall be condemned." The Holy Spirit uses the word "condemned" in reference to being attacked by "weapons." What sort of weapons are these? Some people use physical weapons. Then there are those who use spiritual weapons: the weaponry of words.

Words, once released, begin to work. They do not go anywhere. The only way you can defeat a word spoken against you is to use greater words. Only words can destroy other words. So, when you see yourself trapped, understand that somebody is speaking against you, your marriage, academic life, finances, or family. Such words must be condemned. If you see yourself trapped in a dream, wake up and begin to fight against those words spoken against you using the sword of the Spirit, which is the Word of God.

Witchcraft Activity (Other)

I have provided some examples of dangerous dreams, some of which indicate the presence of witchcraft. Here is a list of other dreams that are a sign of witchcraft activity. If you see any of these things in your dreams, know that something is wrong and trying to work against you.

Crow (Black Bird)

Hyenas

Losing Money

Seeing yourself using the Toilet/Urinating

Seeing yourself in your former high school

Talking Bird (Bird that talks in a dream)

Vomiting

———

You can see, from some of these examples, that certain dreams indicate witchcraft activities. And when I speak of witchcraft, I am talking about a spiritual system that is used to enslave people's spirits or souls. Your soul is comprised of three distinct areas: your mind, your will, and your emotions. You use your mind to think, your emotions to act, and your will to choose. Whatever controls your soul controls how you think, act, and the choices you make. Your spirit contains your consciousness, your intuition, which is also known as your instincts, and the part that has access to God.

The spiritual system of witchcraft is designed to enslave your spirit and soul, the core of who you really are. Once your spirit and soul are captured, the physical person is less likely to achieve, advance, and move forward. Because whatever controls you in the spirit controls you here. Everything that takes place here, in the conscious physical realm, is a reflection of what is taking place or has already taken place or is pending in the realms of the spirit.

Understand that as a Christian, a born-again believer, you cannot be possessed. But that does not mean you cannot be attacked. And the enemy uses what you do not know to attack you. Your ignorance fuels the attack. Dreams are there in the process of growing. But you should not be led by dreams. Notice, I did not say that you should not dream. I said that you should not be led by them. At some point, you should outgrow that method. You should not need to wait until you are asleep to hear from God. That is not the best God has for you. Everywhere you are, every minute, every second, twenty-four hours a day, seven days a week, God wants you to hear what He wants to say to you.

Remember, you are the casting director of your dreams. The images you are familiar with and with which you fill your spirit are what the subconscious mind uses in the "movie." That movie (dream) can be produced by your environment, by God, or in some instances, by the devil.

Dreams are symbolic. And symbols can have multiple meanings. That can make dream interpretation a potential minefield. But if you are led by the Spirit, it is easy for you to know how to manoeuvre. The symbolism, context, and details in the dream, and, most importantly, the leading of the Spirit of God should determine how you interpret a dream. In this final chapter, I will reveal the number one secret to accurately interpreting your dreams. And I will show you how you can take control of your dream life.

SEVEN

TAKE CONTROL OF YOUR DREAMS

"Saddle your dreams before you ride them."

— Mary Webb

Dreams are meant to be understood. But what if there was a better way? What if, instead of just understanding your dreams, you could directly influence the kind of dreams you have? What if there was a way that you could always have good dreams that are inspired by God? It is possible. And I will show you how.

There are some things that you need to understand about the subconscious mind because it is a powerful force and factor in every one of your dreams. The subconscious mind remembers everything. It does not forget because it exists in the spiritual realm, which is a realm of awareness. Every detail that you have observed, knowingly and unknowingly, is stored in your subconscious mind. When you pick up your mobile phone, you see the phone with your eyes. However, your subconscious mind is collecting more information about your phone than you are aware. It is not only recording the shape, colour and model of your phone. It is also recording every detail, down to the screws that hold the phone together.

Here is another important note you need to understand about your subconscious mind. Not only is your subconscious mind a master at collecting and archiving data, but it is also on duty 24-hours a day, 365-days a year, and 366 in a leap year. Your conscious mind works while you are awake and alert. But your subconscious mind works nonstop.

The subconscious mind knows when you are asleep. It seeps an aggregate of what it has curated to the conscious mind so you can have a dream. You might be wondering, what does all of this have to do with you and controlling your dreams? Everything. Because once you understand the power of the subconscious mind and how it works, you will be able to give your subconscious mind correct information before you sleep. And that will directly influence your dreams.

When you have a dream, it is not just the dream that matters. You must also consider your spiritual positioning before the dream. Your previous experience influences your dream. What you do during the day, and more importantly, what you do right before going to bed, matters. Did you pray? Read your Bible or some other book? Did you watch an R-rated movie? What kind of music were you playing? What sort of scriptures did you read? Whatever you read, see, and hear gets into your spirit and become the images in your dream.

There is a previous experience you can maintain so you can have certain kinds of dreams. Spiritually, your environment can talk even when you are quiet. It is like a warm engine that can tell a person has been somewhere even when they are unwilling to talk about it. Information can be extracted from your environment by your spirit. Certain places or environments keep you from understanding the voice of God when He's speaking. Remember Lot? The Bible says his righteous soul was vexed. That causes us to understand that environments can contaminate you and make you think a certain way. So, another vital thing you need to understand is that your environment influences your dreams.

Now, I promised to reveal the number one secret to interpreting your dreams. Of course, all dream interpretation should be by the Spirit of God and skill. But there is a key hidden in Genesis chapter 40, verse 7 and the first part of verse 8, which reads:

And he [Joseph] asked Pharaoh's officers that were with him in the ward of his lord's house, saying, Wherefore look ye so sadly today? And they said unto him, We have dreamed a dream ... (Genesis 40:7-8a)

The context of this verse is a familiar story. Joseph, who is skilled in dreams, is inquiring about his prison mates, the butler and the baker. Each of them has had a dream. When Joseph sees them the following morning, he notices that they are sad. Herein lies the number one secret to interpreting your dreams. When you wake up, the first thing you do is to pay attention to the feeling you had in the dream or immediately upon waking.

Your feelings are crucial. *Every interpretation is based on the feeling you had.* If you dreamt of snakes chasing you and you felt happy, that feeling is the pinnacle of the interpretation. The characters or symbols you saw are secondary. The most important thing is the feeling. Your emotions are the vehicle by which the anointing comes out. If your emotions were happy, regardless of the imagery you saw in the dream, you have to interpret every other part of the dream based on those feelings. *Pay attention to the feeling first.* Everything else flows from that. What I just told you is worth a thousand times more than whatever you paid for this book. I will share a bit more so that you can set the proper environment for your dreams.

There was a disciple that Jesus called that had a noted distinction from all of the other disciples. His name is Nathaniel. As Nathaniel was approaching, Jesus proclaimed, "Behold an Israelite in whom there is no guile." (John 1:47). Jesus was saying that there was no deceit or craftiness in Nathaniel that could be used as a decoy. The problem that you are having with your dreams and their interpretation is you have too many decoys. That statement will not make any sense to you unless you first understand what a decoy is. A decoy is something that is used to lure or entice a person away from an intended course, typically into a trap. This brings me to another vital point. There is an intended course for your dreams.

Dreams are God's idea. When you find yourself having bad dreams, or dreams that give evidence of witchcraft activities or nightmares, it simply means that the devil has gained access to your dreams and corrupted them. But dreams are intended by God to lead you into His purpose (see Job 33, verses 15-17). God draws you to His purpose through dreams. And what does He use to do that? Images.

Understand that the spiritual realm, the realm in which you dream, is a very dark place. You need light to see. Matthew chapter 6 and verse 22 tells us that the light of the body is the eye. It goes on to say that if your eye is "single," then your whole body will be full of light. A "single" eye is not looking at everything. Have you ever seen a jeweller as he examines a diamond? He uses a special eyepiece called a loupe. He will close one eye and look through the loupe with the other eye, focusing on what he needs to see. Similarly, the eye that is "single" is clear and focused on what it needs to see.

In computer programming, there is an acronym, GIGO. It stands for garbage in, garbage out. The GIGO principle applies when it comes to dreams. Why? Because what you put in is what you get out. Dreams use images, and images are based on what you see. That seeing is not always visual. Sometimes it is a seeing that comes by association. That is to say who you are around and the company you keep. The eye is the gate to your spirit. The eye carries images to your mind and your spirit. So, how do you control your dreams? By controlling what you "look at" and the light you use to see.

Never use your culture as a light when it comes to your dreams and the interpretation of them. For example, in your culture, it may be that the colour black is associated with evil. If you interpret your dreams based on that knowledge, you will be using the wrong light. The Bible says that the entrance of God's Word gives light (see Psalm 119, verse 130). That is the light you must use to be able to see your dreams the way God intends. When you use the light of the Word, and see the colour black in a dream, you would have the knowledge that to God there is no difference between light and darkness. King David declared that the darkness and the light are both alike to Him (Psalm 139, verse 12). So, the bottom line is what the Word of God says about the symbols you have dreamt.

Get the Word in you. Jesus said, "The words that I speak unto you, they are Spirit, and they are life." (John 6:63). The Word always creates things, images. The Word gets into you and flushes out the bad images you have. The more Word you have in you, the more light you have, and the better you see. When you can see clearly, there is little to interpret. Things are plain, and you can move from having dreams to dreaming dreams. But that is another subject for another day.

In an earlier chapter, I spoke about dreams that are caused by or because of the people you have around you. That is another kind of light that will influence your dreams and their interpretation. If you want to take charge of your dream life, you must clean your environment. Remove every person who speaks against men and women of God. Block them. You can smile when you see them, but you do not need to be in their quarters.

Separate yourself. How do you separate yourself? Simple. You already know the people who contaminate your spirit. Stay away from them. Get rid of nuisance people who just talk nonsense, even if it's your uncle. Don't allow anyone to contaminate your environment just because they are your relative or friend. Tell yourself, I'm not doing anything that is not of God. Switch off your phone at night. Make a decision that even the devil knows that you are in a space that is different. Leave no decoy for him to corrupt your dream life.

The Bible says, "Bad (evil) company corrupts good manners (character, habits)." (1 Corinthians 15:33). I would go a step further and add, bad company corrupts your dreams. The company you keep makes a difference. That company can be a physical person, but it is not limited to that. It could also be the company you keep on the television or your phone. Be intentional about who you have around you and what you watch and listen to, especially when you are about to go to sleep. Whatever you have around you before you sleep produces images in your subconscious. Your mind carries those images into the dream realm and arranges them to produce a dream. If you have not taken steps to safeguard your environment, your dream can be marred by all kinds of images that you do not want in your dream.

Have you ever wondered why you can watch a horror movie before you sleep and relive it in your dreams? But if you watch a movie with angels, you do not see angels. It is because there is a tipping scale. It is the GIGO principle at work. You have watched too many images that corrupted your dreams. You have listened to too many rumours, gossip, and all kinds of things you thought were interesting. Those kinds of images tip the scale against the images you should have. You must tip the scale in favour of good images if you want to influence your dreams in the right way.

Dreams are about images more than you think. Starting today, read about angels. Read about the angels visiting Zachariah. Read about the angels visiting the mother of Samson. Read about those kinds of things. Whatever you read gets into your spirit and become the images in your dream. Listen to preaching and teaching messages before you go to sleep. Do these things, and you will see a big difference in the quality of your dreams and how you interpret them.

ABOUT THE AUTHOR

Dr Miz Mzwakhe Tancredi is a life architect and a pioneering & leading voice in proclaiming the Gospel of God's grace (Euagellion) with an apostolic and prophetic edge.

Dr Miz is a bestselling author, internationally sought-after conference speaker and global leader. He is a visionary, master dreamer, and highly skilled interpreter of dreams.

Find out more about Dr Miz at
www.mizmzwakhetancredi.org
or on the following social media platforms

f facebook.com/Mizmzwakhetancredi

instagram.com/miz_mzwakhe_tancredi

ALSO BY MIZ MZWAKHE TANCREDI

How to See Angels: The Supernatural Materilizing in the
Natural

Command Your Success

Why Men Fail Women & Why Women Fail Men:
Relationships, Marriage and Sex

Available Now on Amazon.com

Made in United States
Cleveland, OH
26 November 2024

10779966R00049